Backhanded Miracles

Angela Taylor

Presentation by *BookLeaf Publishing*

Web: www.bookleafpub.com

E-mail: info@bookleafpub.com

ISBN: 9789395756679

First edition 2022

DEDICATION

I dedicate this book to all of my amazing doctors and nurses along the way, you all believed in me, even when I didn't.

I dedicate this book to my amazing coworkers who were there on-site that worked with me. Chuck, Judy, Matt, Stan, Caroline and Mila. Also in honor of a fellow brother who I worked with on-site, who has since passed away, I miss you Brad 🩶

I dedicate this book to all my amazing friends and family who stuck by me through it all and still got my back to this day, this is for you! Thanks, I love each and every one of you!

ACKNOWLEDGEMENT

I would like to acknowledge BookLeaf Publishing for hosting this amazing contest! There are SO many talented people out there and they went over and above to help find them and offer this amazing opportunity!

Most of all I'd like to acknowledge my girls, I wouldn't be the mother or person I am today without either of them. They're my number one fans and always there for me, no matter what. Natalia Grand-Maison and Kendra Taylor my love for you is never-ending, love you to the moon and back again! 'More than my own life'

I would also like to acknowledge my nieces, nephews, friends and family for always supporting me and encouraging me to follow this dream of mine.

Also, my Niece, who told me that I should enter this contest, thanks, Tiff!

PREFACE

June 4th 2008 was like any other day. I got up,
got ready and left for work that morning.

Close to coffee break, 10:30 am, my coworkers
couldn't find me, then they heard that someone
was being crushed between a scissor lift and 4"
steel pipes and I-beams. It was me, I had
thousands of pounds of pressure continuously
crushing me, breaking my bones and puncturing
my left lung.

They try to revive me three times and couldn't,
the ambulance left without the lights on, then
someone yelled she's a single mom and has a kid
and they tried one more time and the fourth time
they got a heartbeat.

I was in intensive care in a coma for days and
when I did wake up I didn't know where I was, I
thought I was supposed to be at work and was
going to get in trouble lol. For some reason, I
thought my brother and sister were having a
baby and that's why I was in the hospital. My
mom had to put up daily notes with the day and
the date and reminds me of what happened and

why I was there, kind of like 50 First Dates, the movie.

I sustained all my top ribs being broken with scapulas fractures, my left lung was punctured, both of my clavicles were broken but the one on the left was broken into pieces so I've got a 10-inch plate and eight screws in there. I had a double brachial plexus injury so bad that it paralyzed both of my arms. I had to re-learn how to reuse my arms completely because they were so badly stretched and damaged. I had a huge hematoma on my skull/brain. I'm also slowly going blind from the accident as well, I'm only 44 years old and already legally blind in my left eye. I have struggled long and hard and I've been in therapy for 14 long years now. When they asked me to do a rep of 10, they know that I will do a rep of 40 lol. I have fought long and hard and I will never stop fighting. I refuse to give up on myself too, after all that I have and continue to go through. It's crazy how things affect our bodies in the most incomprehensible ways.

I'd love to include my email in case anyone would like to reach out.

moldette5@icloud.com

I want the tears back that I cried

I want the tears back that I cried,
I sure as hell tried,
To hang onto us,
I thought I had found you, one plus,
To add to our family of two girls and a momma
who hadn't smiled in a while,
When you asked, I walked down that aisle,
I'll always love you for giving to me one more
beautiful girl,
Little toes dancing while she quietly whirls,
A child to bear and love, wrap my arms around
tight and never let go,
But I've now let go of you… I know what I'm
worth now and wouldn't change a thing if I
knew,
Thank you for showing me who I am, just wish
it didn't take this long, to hurt and prolong,
Our little girl didn't have to realize her father
was gone….

I am the woman you fell in love with

Slowly you will see the woman you fell in love
with will shine again,
You weighed me down, I've almost gone insane,
It's ok, I will save myself this time,
I don't need you to know I'm good enough, I've
got mine,
You will regret your decision,
I will no longer run to you...
I love me too!
I deserve more than this, I will come through,
I will rise above this,
You are the one who will miss,
The family you decided to leave,
It's you our girls grieve,
I tried to save us with all my might,
I have a new beginning in sight,
All while you take flight...
You're now living with my best friend and I
hope you're both happy in the end!!

Love's last kiss

You don't want me!?
Then set me free,
Maybe it was never meant to be,
You talk down to and swear at me,
Do you think it's healthy for our daughters to
see,
They will seek in a man what they see in you,
That hurts them SO much when you do,
Make sure this is really what you want,
Your words run in my head with daunt,
What makes you think I'll want you after this?!
Maybe this will be our love's last kiss??

My evil friend

Back here again my evil friend,
Right with me to the bitter end,
Back where we started at square one,
You torture me with your games that are not fun!
Quietly I sit hoping that just for a moment,
you'd go away,
Then you quickly remind me that you're going
to stay,
I hope I can shut you up and out for good,
As anybody in my place would.

Compassion for me?

What I look like and feel like, are two different
things,
Who knows what each passing day will bring,
It's hard to get up and put one foot in front of the
other,
Must move on, my children need their mother,
My body ridden with electric pain waves,
I push myself until my body caves,
I remind myself that I need to care for myself
too,
To slow down, take one task at a time and think
it through,
Better than beating myself up, I'm so good at it,
That frustrates me even more, so I won't make it
a habit,
So each day I get up and put a smile on my face,
It doesn't matter what I feel like, I'm thankful
and give grace

Struggle...

It's hard to tell the difference between day and
night,
Nightmares constantly nagging, leaving me in
fright,
Thoughts that keep coming back,
Break me, I must steer on track,
My mind, once was sharp,
Now feels like it's been warped,
I fight to keep what I have left,
To win these mind struggles that leave me
stressed,
One step forward, two steps back,
Stopped by pain and anxiety attacks,
I will keep going, there's no other way,
Chin up, head high and start fresh everyday!

Nothing left

7

Fuck...I'm a sitting duck,
Unwillingly stuck,
In a rut...what's next?!
Something new.. I can't take anymore,
Kneeling on the floor..
Can't get up...
Just threw up... again,
This is all so mundane... am I going insane?!..yet
Can't catch my breath.. there's nothing left...

Broken but standing

I should have locked myself in my room today
and thrown away the key,
Time to take a step back and really look at me,
My hopes and dreams so far away..just out of
grasp,
I don't want to be that person hiding behind a
mask,
This is me, I am broken and have scars,
But I'm just like the rest of you.. reaching for
stars,
So I guess it's time to show my raw uncensored
self,
Maybe from my courage someone else these
words can help...

Intrusive

I don't want you,
But here you are again, Intrusive memories left
to drive me insane,
Always here, breathing heavy on my neck,
Making my heart pound, hands shake..leaving
me a wreck,
Invading my every thought, at any given
moment,
Leaving me emotionally, mentally, and
physically spent,
These are more than just mere 'thoughts',
They intrude heavily on who I am and what I do,
this is not the life I sought

Looming....

Looming....
Dooming....
Sounds come at me,
Please set me free,
Pounding....
Surrounding....
I'm all by myself,
I need help,
Dreading....
Treading....
In the same spot,
Whether I like it or not,
Hounding....
Frowning....
Another day like this,
My old self I truly miss,
Lying...
Sighing....
I'm good, ok....what a joke,
Feels like I'm going to choke
What was...now broke

Cancer

Cancer, starts with 'can'
Why me dealt this hand,
Things recommended,
Need to heal to be mended,
Some more scars,
Who sets these bars?!
I 'can' fight this too....
Waiting's the hard part, if only the end I knew....

Unleash the Beast

12

Unleash the beast,
The one that fear feeds,
In there deep inside,
Desolation following beside,
I try to hide.....
Isolation...devastation.....my body a donation,
I will fight this beast, bare hand,
Release this tightening band,
Unleash this beast,
Beast is deceased!!

By day, by fright

13

I hate these nightmares my mind creates,
Bombards my mind, even while awake,
Makes me distraught throughout the day,
I try to think of things but these horrors stay,
Leave my mind, body and soul,
As deeper I fall in this nightmarish black hole...

Doing time

Write, write and write some more,
What words to say, my mind torn,
Spill, spill...out they come,
Only get a poem if I catch some,
Concentrate, a little more at a time,
Maybe spit out a rhyme,
Here I sit doing time,
Words all racing around my mind,
Thump, another setback,
So many I can't keep track,
One moment at a time,
No need to look behind,
I'm moving on, this is my choice,
Here I am, hear my voice!

What will happen...

15

What will I do when I'm more dependent,
Here I sit, the lone defendant,
How will I dress,
will I still look my best?
I'll need a driver,
I am a survivor,
I'll learn new ways to do things,
To my other senses, I will cling,
One day yet, they may find a cure,
I'll keep what sight I have left, close and dear

My reality

Tension grips my body throughout,
Throbbing, my head's going to explode, from
the inside out,
Anxiety's got a strong grip on me,
With every extra heartbeat I see,
Nerves sending electric shock waves up and
down,
I do my best to still smile, not frown,
My eyes are a whole other story,
Silently getting harder and harder to see,
Tremble go my hands and my arms,
Twitches and shakes, annoys me but does no
harm,
Pain riddled through my whole body,
This is my reality day after day,
On I march because despite all this I got A LOT
to say!

Spent

17

When I tell you I'm spent,
I'm done, exhausted is what I meant,
I'm done for the day, this body needs rest,
Tomorrow is yet another test,
I don't sleep well at night you see,
Woken by pain and night terror, they won't let
me be,
One more day of aches 'n' pain,
Tomorrow is a new day to do it all over again

Strength

You don't know what strong is,
Until being strong is all you've got,
When you suffer so much, and it never stops,
I don't expect you to know or understand,
I'm the guest of honor to be dealt this hand,
In the blink of the eye,
Only a split second in time,
A life ripped to shreds, leaving me asking why?
But there's no point, there's no rhyme or reason
for this tragedy,
I'm left grieving and longing for the "old me",
Stricken with grief and depression...this can't be
me,
This is when you must fight and resist flight,
Or your gonna miss out on the best parts of your
second chance at life!

Trapped

I feel trapped, there's nowhere to run,
I keep trying to get outta here, this is not fun,
Please, someone...somewhere hear my cries,
I am lost and alone, will this be my demise?!
I can't run or hide from it, always along for the ride,
Making me shake and quiver on the inside,
I sit as still as can be,
In hopes that maybe one day, these feelings will release me

June

How do I keep a smile on my face,
When inside what's left, only feels like a waste,
What in the world has happened to me,
I just want to be the person I used to be,
Just when you think you've had enough,
misfortune comes rolling in,
To have one person afflicted with so much, must
be an evil sin,
I keep moving forward, positive thoughts in
mind,
Even though I feel like I was left behind,
You can break my body, but not my soul,
This battle is not over, yet it's taking its toll,
Every day, I remind myself I'm alive and
thankful to be here,
My nightmares so bad, they'd bring grown men
to tears,
My deepest scars are the ones no one sees,
I put on a brave face to make family feel at ease,
The only way to move is forward, one day at a
time,
I survived this tragedy so I guess this victory is
mine!

Back here again?!

Is it easier to ignore my pain, leave me alone to
dwell..going insane,
Right back where I started, recovery....once
again,
I'll just hide here in this torture and handle it all
alone,
No one can feel it, but they can see it, this pain
I've been thrown,
Is it easier to go away and to let me rest,
Or to be here to support me, is this some kind of
test,
My will feels broken, I'm tired, beat down and
worn,
Must keep going day by day, my emotions
wreaking havoc, piercing like a thorn,
Am I in this all by myself, have I been forgotten
this time around,
Maybe it's easier to pretend we are not back here
once again...
Maybe it's easier if I don't make a sound...
While the pain floats quietly around...